Prayer Journal

This Devotional Journal Belongs To:

_____

Dedication

This Prayer Journal Log book is dedicated to all the people out there who love to record their prayers and document their findings in the process.

You are my inspiration for producing books and I'm honored to be a part of keeping all of your Prayer notes and journals cf organized.

This journal notebook will help you record your details about your prayers.

Thoughtfully put together with these sections to record:

Date, Today's Bible Verse, Today I Am Thankful For, Teach Me To, Prayer Requests, People I Am Praying For Today, and My Answered Prayers.

How to Use this Book

The purpose of this book is to keep all of your Prayer notes all in one place. It will help keep you organized.

This Prayer Journal will allow you to accurately document every detail about recording your prayers. It's a great way to chart your course through journaling your prayers.

Here are examples of the prompts for you to fill in and write about your experience in this book:

1. **Date** - Record the date and time.
2. **Today's Bible Verse** - Write your scriptures for the day.
3. **Today I Am Thankful For** - Log what your gratitude for the day and the things you are thankful & grateful for today.
4. **Teach Me To** - Reflect on what you want the Lord to teach you, your favorite quotes, or any notes from the sermon.
5. **Prayer Requests** - Write notes on your prayer requests.
6. **People I'm Praying For Today** - Record the people you need and like to pray for.
7. **My Answered Prayers** - Log all the prayers that God has answered for you and remind yourself of the power of prayer.

DATE:

Today's Bible Verse:

Dear Heavenly Father,

| *Today, I am thankful for...* | *Teach me to...* |

Prayer Requests

People I'm praying for today...

My answered prayers...

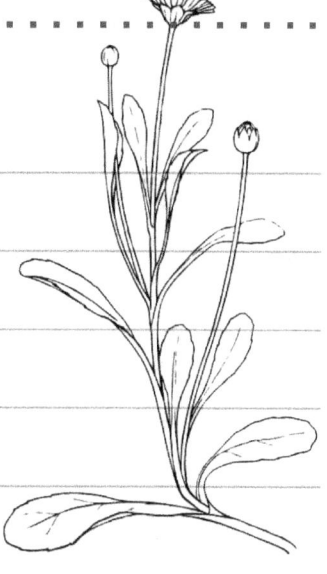

DATE:

Today's Bible Verse:

Dear Heavenly Father,

| *Today, I am thankful for...* | *Teach me to...* |

Prayer Requests

People I'm praying for today...

My answered prayers...

DATE:

Today's Bible Verse:

Dear Heavenly Father,

Today, I am thankful for... | *Teach me to...*

Prayer Requests

People I'm praying for today...

My answered prayers...

DATE:

Today's Bible Verse:

Dear Heavenly Father,

Today, I am thankful for... | *Teach me to...*

Prayer Requests

People I'm praying for today...

My answered prayers...

DATE:

Today's Bible Verse:

Dear Heavenly Father,

| *Today, I am thankful for...* | *Teach me to...* |

Prayer Requests

People I'm praying for today...

My answered prayers...

DATE:

Today's Bible Verse:

Dear Heavenly Father,

Today, I am thankful for... | *Teach me to...*

Prayer Requests

People I'm praying for today...

My answered prayers...

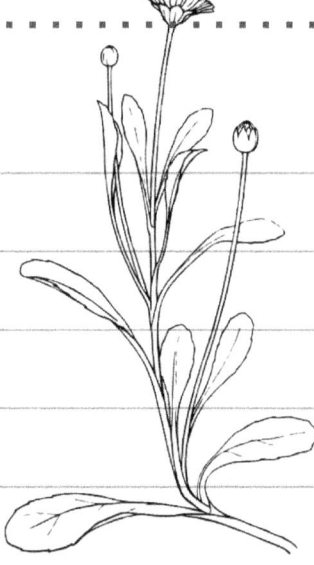

DATE:

Today's Bible Verse:

Dear Heavenly Father,

| *Today, I am thankful for...* | *Teach me to...* |

Prayer Requests

People I'm praying for today...

My answered prayers...

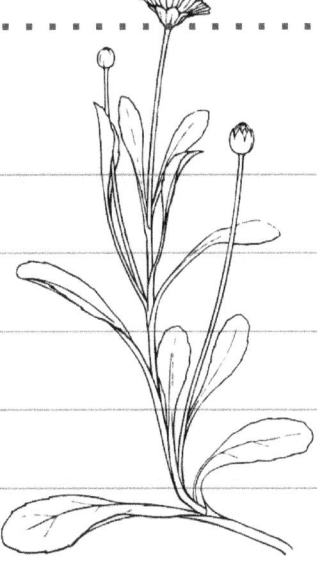

DATE:

Today's Bible Verse:

Dear Heavenly Father,

Today, I am thankful for... *Teach me to...*

Prayer Requests

People I'm praying for today...

My answered prayers...

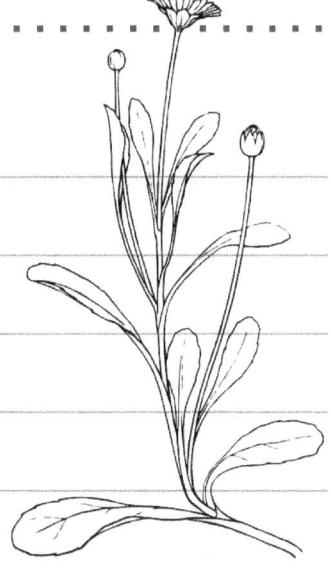

DATE:

Today's Bible Verse:

Dear Heavenly Father,

Today, I am thankful for...	*Teach me to...*

Prayer Requests

People I'm praying for today...

My answered prayers...

DATE:

Today's Bible Verse:

Dear Heavenly Father,

Today, I am thankful for... | *Teach me to...*

Prayer Requests

People I'm praying for today...

My answered prayers...

DATE:

Today's Bible Verse:

Dear Heavenly Father,

| *Today, I am thankful for...* | *Teach me to...* |

Prayer Requests

People I'm praying for today...

My answered prayers...

DATE:

Today's Bible Verse:

Dear Heavenly Father,

Today, I am thankful for... | *Teach me to...*

Prayer Requests

- - - - - - - - - - - - - - - - -

People I'm praying for today...

- - - - - - - - - - - - - - - - -

My answered prayers...

DATE:

Today's Bible Verse:

Dear Heavenly Father,

Today, I am thankful for...	*Teach me to...*

Prayer Requests

People I'm praying for today...

My answered prayers...

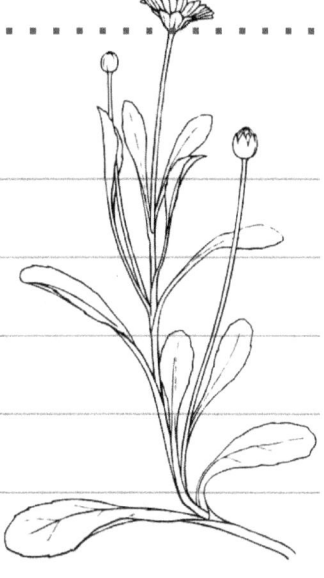

DATE:

Today's Bible Verse:

Dear Heavenly Father,

Today, I am thankful for... | Teach me to...

Prayer Requests

People I'm praying for today...

My answered prayers...

DATE:

Today's Bible Verse:

Dear Heavenly Father,

Today, I am thankful for... | *Teach me to...*

Prayer Requests

People I'm praying for today...

My answered prayers...

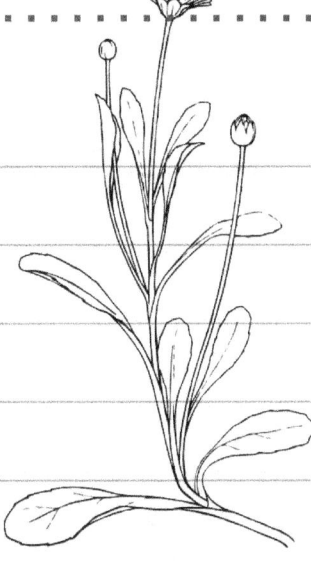

DATE:

Today's Bible Verse:

Dear Heavenly Father,

Today, I am thankful for...	*Teach me to...*

Prayer Requests

People I'm praying for today...

My answered prayers...

DATE:

Today's Bible Verse:

Dear Heavenly Father,

Today, I am thankful for... | *Teach me to...*

Prayer Requests

People I'm praying for today...

My answered prayers...

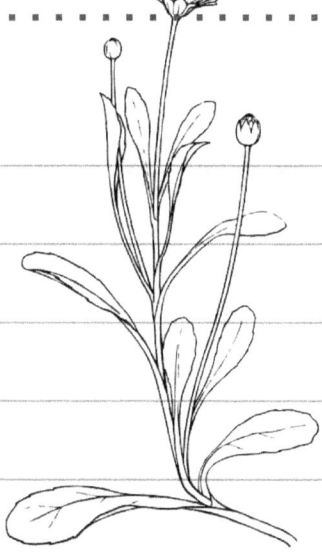

DATE:

Today's Bible Verse:

Dear Heavenly Father,

Today, I am thankful for...

Teach me to...

Prayer Requests

People I'm praying for today...

My answered prayers...

DATE:

Today's Bible Verse:

Dear Heavenly Father,

Today, I am thankful for...   *Teach me to...*

Prayer Requests

People I'm praying for today...

My answered prayers...

DATE:

Today's Bible Verse:

Dear Heavenly Father,

Today, I am thankful for... | *Teach me to...*

Prayer Requests

- -

People I'm praying for today...

- -

My answered prayers...

DATE:

Today's Bible Verse:

Dear Heavenly Father,

Today, I am thankful for... | *Teach me to...*

Prayer Requests

People I'm praying for today...

My answered prayers...

DATE:

Today's Bible Verse:

Dear Heavenly Father,

| *Today, I am thankful for...* | *Teach me to...* |

Prayer Requests

People I'm praying for today...

My answered prayers...

DATE:

Today's Bible Verse:

Dear Heavenly Father,

Today, I am thankful for...	*Teach me to...*

Prayer Requests

People I'm praying for today...

My answered prayers...

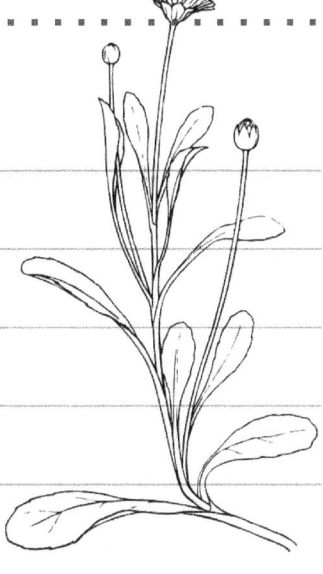

DATE:

Today's Bible Verse:

_____
_____
_____
_____
_____
_____

Dear Heavenly Father,

Today, I am thankful for...	*Teach me to...*

Prayer Requests

People I'm praying for today...

My answered prayers...

DATE:

Today's Bible Verse:

Dear Heavenly Father,

| *Today, I am thankful for...* | *Teach me to...* |

Prayer Requests

People I'm praying for today...

My answered prayers...

DATE:

Today's Bible Verse:

Dear Heavenly Father,

Today, I am thankful for... | *Teach me to...*

Prayer Requests

People I'm praying for today...

My answered prayers...

DATE:

Today's Bible Verse:

Dear Heavenly Father,

Today, I am thankful for... | *Teach me to...*

Prayer Requests

People I'm praying for today...

My answered prayers...

DATE:

Today's Bible Verse:

Dear Heavenly Father,

| *Today, I am thankful for...* | *Teach me to...* |

Prayer Requests

People I'm praying for today...

My answered prayers...

DATE:

Today's Bible Verse:

Dear Heavenly Father,

| *Today, I am thankful for...* | *Teach me to...* |

Prayer Requests

People I'm praying for today...

My answered prayers...

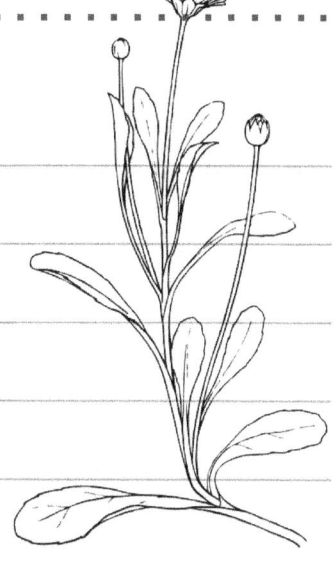

DATE:

Today's Bible Verse:

Dear Heavenly Father,

| *Today, I am thankful for...* | *Teach me to...* |

Prayer Requests

People I'm praying for today...

My answered prayers...

DATE:

Today's Bible Verse:

Dear Heavenly Father,

Today, I am thankful for... | *Teach me to...*

Prayer Requests

People I'm praying for today...

My answered prayers...

DATE:

Today's Bible Verse:

Dear Heavenly Father,

Today, I am thankful for... | *Teach me to...*

Prayer Requests

People I'm praying for today...

My answered prayers...

DATE:

Today's Bible Verse:

Dear Heavenly Father,

Today, I am thankful for... | *Teach me to...*

Prayer Requests

People I'm praying for today...

My answered prayers...

DATE:

Today's Bible Verse:

Dear Heavenly Father,

Today, I am thankful for...

Teach me to...

Prayer Requests

People I'm praying for today...

My answered prayers...

DATE:

Today's Bible Verse:

Dear Heavenly Father,

| *Today, I am thankful for...* | *Teach me to...* |

Prayer Requests

People I'm praying for today...

My answered prayers...

DATE:

Today's Bible Verse:

Dear Heavenly Father,

Today, I am thankful for... | *Teach me to...*

Prayer Requests

People I'm praying for today...

My answered prayers...

DATE:

Today's Bible Verse:

Dear Heavenly Father,

Today, I am thankful for... | *Teach me to...*

Prayer Requests

People I'm praying for today...

My answered prayers...

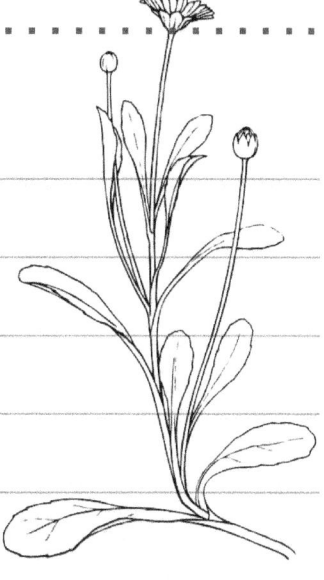

DATE:

Today's Bible Verse:

Dear Heavenly Father,

Today, I am thankful for... *Teach me to...*

Prayer Requests

People I'm praying for today...

My answered prayers...

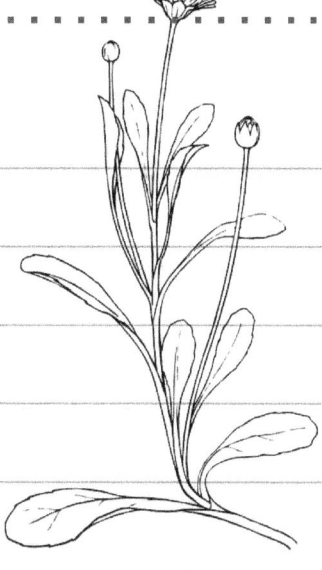

DATE:

Today's Bible Verse:

Dear Heavenly Father,

| *Today, I am thankful for...* | *Teach me to...* |

Prayer Requests

People I'm praying for today...

My answered prayers...

DATE:

Today's Bible Verse:

Dear Heavenly Father,

Today, I am thankful for...   *Teach me to...*

Prayer Requests

People I'm praying for today...

My answered prayers...

DATE:

Today's Bible Verse:

Dear Heavenly Father,

Today, I am thankful for... | *Teach me to...*

Prayer Requests

People I'm praying for today...

My answered prayers...

DATE:

Today's Bible Verse:

Dear Heavenly Father,

Today, I am thankful for...	*Teach me to...*

Prayer Requests

- -

People I'm praying for today...

- -

My answered prayers...

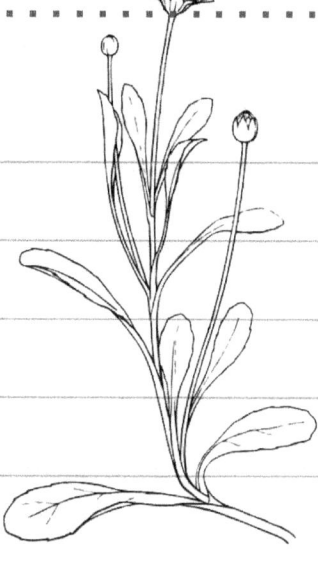

DATE:

Today's Bible Verse:

Dear Heavenly Father,

| *Today, I am thankful for...* | *Teach me to...* |

Prayer Requests

People I'm praying for today...

My answered prayers...

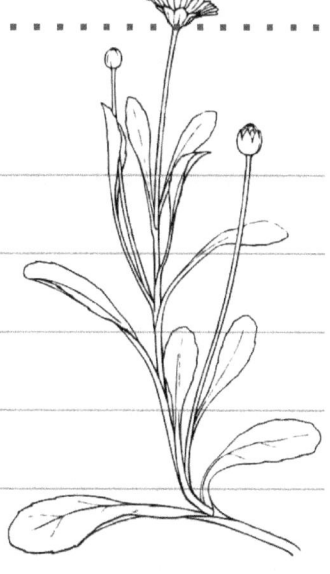

DATE:

Today's Bible Verse:

Dear Heavenly Father,

Today, I am thankful for... | *Teach me to...*

Prayer Requests

People I'm praying for today...

My answered prayers...

DATE:

Today's Bible Verse:

Dear Heavenly Father,

Today, I am thankful for...   *Teach me to...*

Prayer Requests

People I'm praying for today...

My answered prayers...

DATE:

Today's Bible Verse:

Dear Heavenly Father,

Today, I am thankful for...	*Teach me to...*

Prayer Requests

People I'm praying for today...

My answered prayers...

DATE:

Today's Bible Verse:

Dear Heavenly Father,

Today, I am thankful for...   *Teach me to...*

Prayer Requests

People I'm praying for today...

My answered prayers...

DATE:

Today's Bible Verse:

Dear Heavenly Father,

Today, I am thankful for...	Teach me to...

Prayer Requests

People I'm praying for today...

My answered prayers...

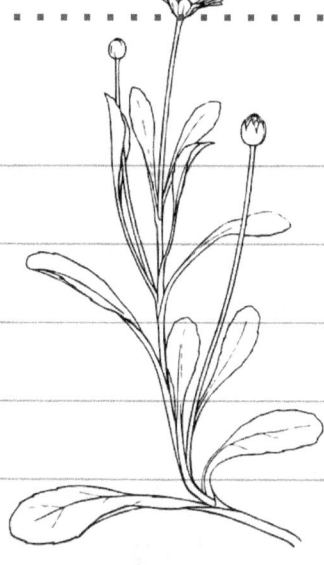

DATE:

Today's Bible Verse:

Dear Heavenly Father,

Today, I am thankful for... | *Teach me to...*

Prayer Requests

People I'm praying for today...

My answered prayers...

www.ingramcontent.com/pod-product-compliance
Lightning Source LLC
Chambersburg PA
CBHW071406080526
44587CB00017B/3186